Treasures Gained in This Land

One missionary's life in Japan

Ruth Dueck

Siretona Creative
Calgary, Alberta, Canada

Copyright © 2021 by Ruth Dueck
First Edition — April 2021

Originally written in Japanese by Ruth Dueck,
Asahikawa, Japan, March 2016

English translation by Ruth Dueck,
Winnipeg, MB, Canada, Winter 2021

All rights reserved.

978-1-988983-22-6 (Paperback)
978-1-988983-23-3 (eBook)

Short portions of the author's words may be quoted without permission,
but should be credited.

No part of this publication may be reproduced in any form, or by any
means, electronic or mechanical, including photocopying, recording, or any
information browsing, storage, or retrieval system, without permission in
writing from the publisher.

Bible references from New International Version (NIV)
unless otherwise noted.

Cover Design by Colleen McCubbin

Produced by Siretona Creative, Calgary, AB, Canada
www.siretona.com

Distributed to the trade by The Ingram Book Company

Contents

Prologue	4
Treasures Gained Through Knowing God's Faithfulness	7
Through His Leading	8
Through My Family	11
Through My Parents' Deaths	14
Treasures Gained Through Human Relationships	19
Through Fellow Missionaries	20
Through the Japanese Church	25
Treasures Gained Through Difficulties	43
When Things Didn't Go as Planned	44
When Betrayed	46
When I Hit the Wall of My Own Limits	48
Treasures Gained Through Seeing God at Work	51
Turning to God in Their Final Hours	52
When Prayer Was Answered	58
When the Impossible Became Possible	60
Closing	64
Acknowledgements	67
Author Biography	68

Prologue

My 42 years in Japan seemed to fly by in some ways and in other ways they felt like a long, long time. How do you put 42 years into a small book? Pastor Komido, a fellow pastor, was a great support and encourager in the process. I felt I didn't have the time, but he kept at me with phone calls asking "Have you started writing yet? How far have you come in your homework? How's your book coming along?" These weekly calls began to cause me fret and loss of sleep. So, I asked the Lord, "What do You want me to do? Please show me. Tomorrow morning after my quiet time and breakfast I will go to my computer and pray for Your leading." You can imagine my utter surprise the next morning when the thoughts just flowed! Six hours later I had the concept for the book, the title, chapter headings, and the first chapter written. I knew then I had to write it. I first wrote the book in Japanese to give to my friends, fellow workers, and the six churches that I had pioneered as a farewell gift. Out of 500 books, I came back to Canada with 36 books after two and a half months.

Going back and remembering God's faithfulness and care for me over the years was a good discipline and it was a real joy to be reminded of how the Lord had worked over the 42 years. Through writing down these reflections, I have come to a new and fresh appreciation of God's love. I thank Him from the bottom of my heart.

Writing this book in Japanese, I knew I would need a Japanese friend who would edit it for me. In answer to prayer God led me to Izu. She and her husband were on the same orientation course as I was in Singapore when we started our missionary journey 42 years ago. When I went down to Tokyo for mission business, I made a point to see them. She read my first few chapters and said, "Ruth, I would love to do this for you. I am looking forward to reading your story myself in the process." Thank you, Izu san.

My prayer is that this little book will be a chance for you to see God's faithfulness and discover for yourself some of the treasures that He has given you.

**Ruth Dueck
member of OMF International**

Visiting with Pastor Komido and his wife and a friend

Treasures Gained Through Knowing God's Faithfulness

Through His Leading

"For I know the plans I have for you," declares the Lord, "plans to prosper you and not to harm you, plans to give you hope and a future." (Jeremiah 29:11)

After high school two friends and I shared an apartment in Steinbach, Manitoba and started a life of fun and enjoyment. Every day I was busy with work and hobbies. Each night was a different activity—curling twice a week, sewing classes, and youth group at church to name a few. I loved the freedom of being away from home making some money and enjoying fun times with friends. One day in February we planned to go to the Russian circus on ice which was coming to Winnipeg. We decided to make it an outing with friends. Six of us would go together in one car. My friends both did not have a driver's licence, but I did. The problem was that I did not have a car, but I wasn't worried. My older brother would most certainly lend me his car as he usually did when I needed it. However, when I asked him this time, things were different. He said an adamant "No." I was surprised and thought, Oh well, I'll just keep asking and surely he will change his mind. But I was wrong. He stuck to his guns. He did not give in even though I put the pressure on hard. In the end I had to give in. I decided to ask my dad, but he too said "No." What would I tell my friends? They were depending on me.

Finally, two days before the circus on ice, I told my friends my predicament. "I'm sorry but my brother will not lend me his car." To my surprise my friends were not upset.

They said, "Oh that's okay. We have a different car." Then there was an awkward silence and they said, "But there is no room for you."

They got a different car and with it they got another driver. I was stunned. What on earth was this? Why had I bothered fighting with my brother the way I did? And why would my friends reject me like this? On the day of our outing, after my friends had left for the Ice Capades, I called my spiritual friend and told her my story.

"To be honest I'm not surprised," she said, "but at the same time this did not happen to you by chance. I believe God allowed it for a purpose. Now you have the homework to try and find out what that purpose is, don't you?"

After hanging up the phone I turned to my Bible and opened the place I had read that morning. It was Isaiah 41. I read the passage again. This time the words were powerful and impressed me deeply.

> "You are my servant;
>   I have chosen you and have not rejected you.
>   So do not fear, for I am with you;
>   do not be dismayed for I am your God.
> I will strengthen you and help you;
>   I will uphold you with my righteous right hand. …
>   For I am the Lord, your God,
>   who takes hold of your right hand
>   and says to you, Do not fear;
>   I will help you."

In that moment God taught me a deep lesson about His faithfulness. Your friends and people around you might let you down, but God NEVER will. He is always near and protects His own. I am imperfect and may even turn my back on Him, but God will never leave me. This is the God who calls me His servant and He has chosen me! As I thought about that I realized that if He has called me to be His servant then I'd better prepare to serve Him. That night I made a huge decision that would change my life forever: in fall I would quit my job in insurance and go to Bible School.

When I got to work the next day, I went over to my boss's desk and told him that I would be quitting after the summer because I was going to Bible School.

"Why are you telling me this now in February? There are another seven months till September!"

I probably did it so that I wouldn't change my mind. From that day on I knew that I would eventually be serving my Creator, the One who chose me as His own, full-time. However, as time passed, everyday things started to be more pressing. By May of that year my dream and commitment started to waver. Did I really need to go that far in my commitment? I told the Lord "I'm sorry but I'm a person of little faith. I'm beginning to doubt my decision. If that was really You speaking to me in February, then please show me again from the book of Isaiah. I will read from chapter 41 to the end. If nothing speaks to me, I will change my plans."

I sat down and started reading at Isaiah 41. Nothing seemed to be speaking to me or challenging me. Slowly I began to think, Well maybe I really don't need to go the extent that I thought. Just then God spoke: "You will go out in joy and be led forth in peace; the mountains and hills will burst into song before you, and all the trees of the field will clap their hands." Now I knew that He was indeed leading me to continue the path that I had started. From that time on there was a seed of interest in my heart, but it was a secret.

That fall I started my three years of training at Millar College of the Bible in Saskatchewan. For me it was the perfect place to train for my future ministry. While at Millar I was exposed to the needs of the world. Every week we would meet together in small groups to pray for different countries around the world. Since childhood I had been exposed to Japan and found it an intriguing country. So my first choice naturally would have been to be in the group that would be praying for Japan, but somehow, I felt that I should not make my choice known. In that case I would be placed in the group where numbers were low. When I looked at the bulletin board a week later, I found I had been placed in the Africa prayer group. My heart sank within me. I had no desire to work in Africa. Not only that, but Africa was the one place that I definitely did not want to go to. An amazing thing happened in me that year. My prejudice toward Africa was completely taken away as I became pen pal friends with a family serving there.

Even so, the desire for Japan was still strong in my heart. In my second year I prayed, "Lord if this desire is from You then please lead the women's dean to put my name in the Japan prayer group without me saying anything to anyone." Two weeks later when I looked at the list on the bulletin board my name was not only in the Japan prayer group, but I was leader of the group. From that day forward I was very intentional in my preparation to go to Japan.

I was also challenged in reading Hudson Taylor's Spiritual Secret and decided that I wanted to work with a mission like that. It was amazing to see how they would work together in teams and in faith. For me OMF International was that mission. On June 21, 1974 I left Canada and went to Singapore for orientation to Asia and then on to Japan. I had just turned 23 when I left for Asia. Sensing God's clear leading each step of the way was a real strength and encouragement to me.

Through My Family

"May your father and mother be glad; may she who gave you birth rejoice." (Proverbs 23:25)

I was born into a Christian home. We were 10 siblings. I was the oldest girl and had one older brother, three younger sisters, and five younger brothers. From a young age I was caring for younger brothers and sisters. I also had many jobs around the house to perform. From age 10 I was given the responsibility to bake bread and buns for our family every Saturday. If it was bread it was between 12 and 15 loaves. If it was buns, it was about 400 to 450 at a time. There was no end to the jobs that needed to be done in such a large family.

At the age of ten another major event happened in my life. One night we were driving home from grandma and grandpa's house. Everyone was tired after a fun day, so most of my siblings were asleep. The radio caught my ear and I listened intently to the program that was on. It was Back to the Bible. Even though I was born into a Christian home, that faith had not yet become my own. So, when we got home and inside the house I said to my mother, "Mom I know that if Jesus would come tonight, I would not be ready to go to heaven. How can I trust Him as my Saviour?"

She called my dad and said, "Take Ruth aside. She has an important matter to discuss with you."

He took me into their bedroom, and I told him, "I want to trust Jesus as my Saviour. What do I do?" He knelt with me beside their bed and opened his Bible to John 3:16. He read it to me: "For God so loved the world that He gave His one and only Son, that whoever believes in Him shall not perish but have eternal life." He went on to explain what this verse meant and then led me in a prayer of repentance and faith: "Lord Jesus I am not a good person but a sinner. You died on the cross for me and for my sin. Thank you. From now on I want to live as your child. Please lead me as Your child." From that day on I knew that I was God's child and lived in that joy.

However, six years later I was reminded that I still had sin in my life that I was trying to hide from other people. At six years of age I had stolen a small hand mirror from the neighbourhood store owned by Uncle Levi. To hide what I had done, I had buried the mirror in the ground so that no one would know. I never used that mirror even once. Of course, neither my mother nor my father knew about this. That night the Holy Spirit did not let me sleep. Time after time I went down to the bathroom. After two or three trips Mom asked, "Who's there?"

"It's me, Ruth" I said.

"Are you not feeling well?" she asked.

I replied that I was fine, but a few minutes later I was down again. This time she got up and came to check on me. "Are you really, okay? What's wrong?"

Finally, I could not hold back any longer. With tears I told her what I had done. She said to me, "Tomorrow morning before school you write a letter and apologize to Uncle Levi and tell him what you did. Dad is going to work later tomorrow so he can deliver the letter ."

The next morning, I got up early and wrote my letter. I went to school with a load off my back that day. My dad took the letter to Uncle Levi. That night a visitor came to see me—Uncle Levi. He thanked me for my letter, gave me a big hug and said, "I forgive you." He promised to pray for me as I would go forward and follow Jesus. Through this experience I learned an important lesson about confessing our sin and receiving God's forgiveness.

I thank God for my parents and my siblings. Through them I have come to know God's love and faithfulness. One of my sisters and one brother and his family visited me in Japan. My parents also came twice. These visits helped me to realize that my family was part of my life in Japan. On another occasion, when my position changed drastically from missionary to being called as pastor of Midori ga Oka church, my family celebrated with me and bought a suit for me to wear at the installation ceremony. I thank God for my family even though most of my adult life I was far removed from their world.

Through My Parents' Deaths

"A man's steps are directed by the Lord. How then can anyone understand his own way?" (Proverbs 20:24)

One Friday afternoon just before Christmas I had a strange telephone call from my mother. "I've called today because I wanted to hear your voice one last time. The end of my journey on this earth is near."

"What are you saying mom? Are you okay? Do you have peace?"

She replied, "I am fine and I have peace in my heart. But I don't think I will see you again on this earth. Please make sure you look out for dad."

That was just after lunch on Friday, December 21, 2008. I was perplexed and shaken up by this call. I contacted family but they assured that she was still fine and I did not need to worry. However, as I prayed about the phone call and thought about my mother's words, I knew that I should try to get back to Canada as soon as possible. We had our church's Christmas candlelight service on the 24th with a cello concert and the cellist was staying with me. That Friday, late afternoon, I went to the travel agent to book my ticket. By 5:30 I had the ticket in hand and two days later was back in Canada. I went straight to the nursing home when I got back to Canada even though it was after 9 pm.

When I walked into Mom's room she turned around and said, "Ruth, you came!" and held my hand tightly.

After about ten minutes I said, "I should go and say hello to Dad."

"Oh no," she said. "This is our time." And so we kept on talking. I had another five days with her before she went to be with the Lord.

Caring for elderly parents is very important in South East Asia. I was very aware that I had not been able to be present at many of the events in our family over the years. These five days with her were a special gift from God.

During these days we got to talk about the things that concerned her. There had been a situation in her family where her aunts had been jealous of the inheritance that her father received from his parents. She wondered how she would deal with any bad feelings when she met them in heaven. She looked forward to seeing her father and also her aunts, but worried her father would be hurt if she was too friendly with her aunts or vice versa. I could assure her that she did not need to worry about that. In heaven there will be no sad times, only forgiveness and joy. After we prayed together, she was filled with joy and had no further worries about the situation.

Two days later she said to me, "I don't know what it will be like when I get to the border of heaven." In her youth she had worked in the fruit canneries in Niagara on the Lake, Ontario. She was originally from the

United States, and one day she and a group of friends went over the border for a meal. All was well until they were heading back to Canada. The immigration officer did not want to let her through because she did not have her passport with her. This experience made her wonder what it would be like at the border between earth and heaven. I assured her, "God Himself is looking after everything. And He makes no mistakes. Would you like me to pray and ask Him to look after all the details for you?"

"Do you think we can do that?"

"Sure," I said. "Let's pray."

Mom became filled with peace and joy at the prospect of very soon meeting her Saviour, Jesus Christ.

Three years later, on December 30, 2011, at 4:00 in the morning I had a call from my sister saying that dad was in his last hours—maybe another six or so hours. I quickly packed my bags. As soon as the shops opened, I went to the travel agent to get my ticket to go back to Canada. Flights are almost impossible to get over New Year's in Japan. When the agent checked available flights to Tokyo there were none available, and only 2 seats left from Tokyo to Vancouver. I prayed. The agent checked every airport in Hokkaido, the northern island, but every flight was fully booked.

Finally, she looked at me and said, "Well, what do you want to do?"

I said, "Well, I can't swim to Tokyo."

Just then a girl in the back piped up saying, "There's just been a first-class cancelation on a flight from Sapporo to Tokyo."

I said I would take that ticket, raced home to park my car, get my bags and stop at the bank to get money to pay for my ticket. I took a taxi to the travel agent, went in to pick up the tickets, and then took the two-hour express train to the airport in Sapporo. I had just enough time for a drink in the first-class lounge before I boarded my plane. In Tokyo I transferred from one airport to the other on a 2-hour limousine bus ride. Because the time was very tight, the ticket agent had advised me to call the Air Canada counter every 20 minutes to tell them where I was on the express highway. I walked up to the Air Canada counter just as they were closing. I made it just in time!

From the Winnipeg Airport I went straight to the nursing home where my dad was. When I walked into the room, he opened his eyes and recognised me although he could no longer speak. The chaplain at the home had told our family that my father had expressed regret the day before because he felt he had shortchanged his children in different ways. We decided that we should each take time to let him know that we didn't hold any grudges against him. At noon, while most of the family went out for a bite to eat, my sister and I sat with him singing "When we all get to heaven." In the middle of the second verse his eyes rolled upward and he was with Jesus.

Over the years I was in Japan I had not been able to be with family for weddings, special celebrations and so forth. The Lord allowed me to be with both of my parents when they went to meet their Redeemer. God was faithful in directing the timing and managing every detail necessary in these special times.

My parents David and Katherine

Treasures Gained Through Human Relationships

Through Fellow Missionaries

"And how can they preach unless they are sent? As it is written, '"How beautiful are the feet of those who bring good news."' (Romans 10:15)

At the time of this writing there were approximately 130 missionaries working in Japan with OMF International. They came to Japan from Singapore, Korea, Hong Kong, Philippines, New Zealand, Australia, America, Canada, England, Scotland, Ireland, Wales, Brazil, Switzerland, Germany, and Uganda—over a dozen different countries with their own unique cultures and languages. You might wonder, "How could these people ever unite and become one in goals, mission and commitment?" Humanly speaking it was a miracle - but it was and still is a reality!

We all came with different backgrounds in work and ministry as well. At any given time you might find the following specialists among us: doctor, nurse, accountant, musician, engineer, jewelry designer, lawyer, teacher, theologian, linguist, interior designer, dancer, museum curator, snowboard instructor, pharmacist, computer programmer, actor, and secretary, among others. How could such a diverse bunch of people ever come together and work toward the same goal? As we set Christ and His desires as our priority it was amazing what could be accomplished. We worked together in Japan doing church planting, supporting the work with many unique ways of outreach and evangelism. In Japan less than one per cent of the population are Christian. We needed to use every opportunity and gift we had as a means to make Jesus Christ known.

Even with such a rich heritage we were a family. We had an annual conference when we met together to learn together from God's Word, and for fun and fellowship. It was amazing what we could all come up with, and it was not uncommon to cry from laughter. We also encouraged each other as family. We circulated a monthly letter, listing our specific prayer needs, which enabled us to pray more effectively for each other. At Christmas and birthdays, we celebrated in smaller groups. My contribution to our Christmas party was usually a turkey and home baked cookies. If anyone in our families in our homelands were in need or hurting, we would pray for each other. These were a few of the ways in which we cared for and encouraged each other.

Personally, I had two very close friends in this large family: Irene, who came to Japan from Scotland, and Ingrid, who joined the work from Germany. In my 42 years in Japan we shared many experiences together. Sometimes Japanese people would wonder how we could ever become so close and supportive of one another considering our differences. They would often shake their heads saying, "I don't get it. How do they get on so well?" After all, we were all strong-minded enough to have left our own cultures and families behind. My Swiss friend Jeanne said at one of our parties, "OMF is like Swiss chocolate. Usually, it is just the right sweetness, but once in a while it tastes a little too sweet." I am so thankful for the privilege I have had of sharing life with these dear friends.

Forty-seven years ago, in 1974 I went to Singapore for orientation at our International Headquarters. There were 22 people from 11 different countries in our orientation group. One couple from Japan left an indelible impression on my life.

Makino sensei had attended Discipleship Training Center in Singapore previously, so he had many friends that he was constantly in contact with by phone. I was amused that he always repeated, "Hi, Hi" in Japanese on the telephone and laughed. Later I found out it meant, "Yes, yes." He was the oldest person on our course and I was the youngest. He loved to tell jokes and be the center of the party. His wife Izu, on the other hand, brought him down to earth and was a very caring helper and caregiver. She made a small booklet of Japanese words that I would need when I got to Japan. With the words she drew little pictures. These greetings and basic words were very helpful to me on the 20-hour train trip from Tokyo to Hokkaido. These two were a very precious older brother and older sister to me.

Let me share a little more about my two closest friends. Irene and I went on yearly holidays together for the last 30-some years of my time in Japan. Japan has 47 prefectures and each year we would sit down and plan which prefectures we would visit that year. I had a car and so we would plan our holiday and go.

Japan is comprised of four main islands so often our trip would involve ferry rides, some of which were 24 or more hours long. One time we were separated, as the passengers had to board by walking across the ramp while the driver drove the car onto the lower deck. We then had to go up to top deck to the beds that we'd booked. The man in charge of guiding the drivers outside guided me to the wrong line so Irene left on the ferry without me. She was waiting for me to come up, but I never showed. Finally, she was able to convince the staff that something was very wrong. About an hour after our ferry should have left, I was still waiting in line. I thought this was very strange for Japan as they were usually very quick to let you know if something was wrong. I suddenly saw four men coming toward my car. They informed me that they had put me in the wrong line up and my ferry had already left. Fortunately, I was in an express ferry line, and even though I left two hours later than Irene I arrived five hours earlier. The ferry company paid for all our meals throughout the journey and a hotel room for me upon arrival.

Another time Ingrid, Irene, and I went on holiday to a famous resort area in the mountains north of Tokyo. Partway into the 6-hour trip through one of the five-kilometer tunnels in the mountains, we realized that we were falling behind the rest of the traffic and our car was slowing down. We were finally able to turn in to a rest site. We got out and looked. We had had a blowout! We started with removing all our luggage from the trunk. Finally, we dug out the spare tire. We started changing the tire while Irene ran around with her camera making sure that we had a record of all that had happened.

These different times are happy reminders of our friendship and God's goodness to us. The day came when Ingrid told us that she would be getting married. Certainly, our lives changed, but our friendship did not. Ingrid asked me to make the wedding cake for her. These two have been very special friends over the years. I dreaded to think what it would be like when I left Japan, but they have both come to visit me in Canada.

Three years before my retirement, I was asked to serve as the Hokkaido director for OMF for one year. This gave me the opportunity to interact with many of our new missionaries. It was especially precious for me to mentor two young singles. One of them, Hoi Yan, lived in the same city as I did and once a month, we would go to one of the many hot springs in our area to relax and talk. This was always a special time. The other, Fanny, was from Hong Kong. She and I also had many opportunities to share with each other how God was working in our lives.

I thank God for the many friendships and relationships with different missionaries. Each one is a very special treasure to me from God.

Missionary fellowship

My buddies, Irene and Ingrid

OMF Hokkaido team

Through the Japanese Church

"As iron sharpens iron, so one man sharpens another." (Proverbs 27:17)

I was privileged to serve in six churches in the pioneer church planting stages. Each of these churches were unique opportunities to know God deeper. Let me share with you some of these unique experiences in each place.

Kuroishi

I had just finished one year of Japanese language study and a six-month stint working in the mission office. Normally new missionaries would have two years of language and culture study before being sent out to their first ministry assignment. That gives you an idea of the urgency of my initial placement. I was sent to Kuroishi, in the northern part of Japan's main island, with Judy, an English missionary who had finished her two years of language study.

The church had been started by senior missionaries who had to return home due to health and family concerns. There was no one to preach on Sundays other than Judy or me. Neither of us had experience writing Japanese sermons and did not feel ready to do so. We decided rather than preaching we would prepare Bible studies. We could ask questions and the church people could answer, even though often we did not understand the answers. Usually we had between eight and twelve people attend on a Sunday morning. We decided to study the book of Philippians.

We knew that this was not a long-term placement for either of us, and wondered how we could make the most of this placement. There were usually three young people in the service. Two of them were high schoolers and they were both Christians. We decided that our abilities and gifts would be best suited to focusing on high schoolers. We started by having both the girls join us every Sunday afternoon for a time of prayer and planning. We decided to start Young Club every Friday night. We prayed that God would open this door for us. The two young Christian girls were excited at the prospect of us doing something for youth. How should we start such a ministry? They were able to let us know about special events happening at school and give us input regarding scheduling. We were excited to see what God would do.

We made 1200 flyers, with the girls' help, planning to hand them out at the school gate on Wednesday, two days before our first meeting. Wednesday morning, Judy and I stared in disbelief at the hardest, heaviest rain shower we had ever experienced. We prayed at breakfast and again before we left the house that God would stop the rain, because if it continued students probably would not take the flyers. We didn't have a car, but we had bicycles. We put on our rain ponchos and wrapped the flyers in three layers of plastic bags. When Judy and I got to the school gate we were both drenched, but as we got off our bikes, the rain stopped abruptly. We were both stunned. God had answered our prayers.

We handed out our flyers and students saw that we were young so immediately tried their English on us. Our flyers disappeared quickly, and just as we handed out the last one, the fierce rain started as abruptly as it had stopped. Judy and I went home amazed and so thankful for God's miraculous intervention. I realized through this experience that you can trust God with the little things and the big things that are so far beyond our control. Students started to come to our Young Club. Each week we had between 15 and 20 high school students for games, Bible times, and snacks. The two young girls that helped us later went to Bible school to prepare for full-time Christian work.

Because Kuroishi was the first Japanese church for me to serve in, everything was new and exciting. Especially after seeing how God could stop the rain, I looked forward to the other adventures He would have for us. By our third month in Kuroishi we felt like we had found our footing so we wanted to do another outreach. This time we reached out to all age groups with the movie Shiokari Pass, which was written by a Japanese Christian. We rented the local town hall, which seated about 300 people. We prepared flyers, posters, and tickets, and set forth. The task of going door to door to invite people was tedious. Everywhere people said "Iketara ikimasu," which means "If we can possibly go, we'll be there." This was the literal translation, but in actual fact these two words were a very polite way of saying, "We probably won't come." We were sure that our hall would be crowded and then what would we do? Would you believe, on the actual night seven people showed up for the movie? I was sure that Japanese people couldn't be trusted if they could tell an outright lie like that and think that was alright. I soon learned that they were just being polite in their refusal.

An elderly couple, Mr. and Mrs. Matsuoka, were the faithful base of that church. They committed themselves to pray for us and the work that was going on. Mr. Matsuoka was bedridden and so prayer was his work. He took it very seriously. They also looked out for us, these strange foreigners. Although Mrs. Matsuoka looked after us, her bedridden husband, and many other people who came to the church, I never once heard her complain about things.

These were the very valuable lessons I learned in my first placement. God can be trusted and He is faithful! These are certainly some very special treasures.

Kita Hiroshima

This beddotaun (literally "bedtown" or bedroom community as we might call it in Canada) of Sapporo on the northern island was my second placement. This church plant was begun by two single missionaries, Mabel and Lotte, one year before I arrived there. They started the work from nothing! Mabel and a co-worker had led a couple, Mr. & Mrs. Miyahara, to faith in a previous church plant. The couple built a big new house in Kita Hiroshima where they planned to live in their retirement about three years down the road. In the meantime, they wanted the missionaries to live in their new house and start a work from there.

The first people introduced to Mabel and Lotte were Mrs. Shiromoto, who was introduced by a radio evangelist, and Mrs. Ishigaki, who was introduced by an evangelist from Hokuei Church in Sapporo. These two ladies were very keen to find out what the Bible said and they wanted to know Jesus Christ. However, both of their husbands opposed their faith strongly, even going as far as to tear up their Bibles on more than one occasion, and forbidding them to see "those missionaries." Mr. Shiromoto would phone his wife throughout the day to check if she had gone out. Mr. Ishigaki would lock his wife up in the half-bath when it came time for church on Sunday morning. In spite of this, both women still managed to come.

Later Mr. Kurozawa and Mrs. Soga also became seekers, then came to faith and were baptized on the confession of their faith. Mrs. Shiromoto and Mrs. Ishigaki were baptized earlier. When the Miyaharas came to live in

Kita Hiroshima there were already four believers. As they moved in, Mabel and I moved out to the red brick house in the area. We called it the Bible House. One of the stipulations in Kita Hiroshima was that church buildings were not allowed in the housing development. As long as we called it Bible House instead of referring to it as a church, we were free to host our kids' club, Bible studies, outreach and worship services.

Many people came to this place to hear the gospel. Saturdays at 1:30 in the afternoon we had kids' club with 35 to 50 children attending weekly. The road in front of our house was packed with bicycles for two hours during that time, but neighbours never complained. We didn't have a meeting room as such so we would clear all the furniture out of our living room each week and put it into my bedroom. Mrs. Ishigaki and Mrs. Shiromoto were both early childhood educators and were invaluable as they helped with that outreach.

We tried many different ways to share the Good News of Jesus Christ with people. Once a month we had a meeting called "At Home." For this meeting we usually tried to get a Japanese pastor to come from Sapporo to give the message. We would also plan for a testimony and served coffee and snacks. We invited contacts we had met over the previous month. This too was a very informal meeting, and the living room furniture once again made the trip to my bedroom. This was the first time I served alongside Japanese pastors.

After my fellow missionaries returned to Canada and Switzerland to retire, I worked with the Japanese pastor, Mr. Kishimoto, and his family. I learned so many things from him. I was especially surprised by the detail of his hand-made Bible study books. It taught me how much Japanese people pay attention to details and want to talk things through many times before they commit to moving forward with something. For me it was a precious lesson learned.

I gained these and so many more precious treasures here.

Otaru

When my friend Ingrid's fellow worker returned home to Australia, I was asked to join Ingrid in the work in Otaru, a port city in Hokkaido. We lived together on the second floor of the church building. In Otaru I was introduced to working with university students. I taught English conversation at the Otaru City Hospital Nursing School and at the Otaru Commerce National University. Jan from England, who had been teaching there, told me, "You'll do fine. I never had more than 25 students in any class and Michael, a full-time teacher from America, will always help you if you ask him." She also introduced me to two OMF missionaries who could coach me and give me advice when I needed it.

On opening day, each of us presented a mock class for potential students and their friends. The students were then given the option to choose which teacher's class they wanted to be a part of. I was astonished to hear that 72 students signed up for one of my classes and 69 for the other. To be honest, I did panic for a moment. I had never even attended university myself. I only had an Evangelical Teacher Training Association certificate from Millar, but I was young and liked challenges so this would be God's opportunity. There was a limit to the amount of evangelism I could do in class. I could explain the true meaning of Christmas and Easter and so forth, but not much more, so I invited any students who were interested to an English class at my house. In that year, every aspect of what I had learned so far was put to the test. I loved it.

I was still involved in the church work of preaching, Bible studies, etc. Once a month, Ingrid and I would go to Shakotan, a town one and a half hours along the coast from us, for a short worship time and lunch with a believer who could only make the trip to Otaru once every three or so months because she had no vehicle. These trips were a blessing to both Ingrid and myself. The road to Shakotan featured beautiful rock formations along the coastline. I never got tired of seeing them. The drive there and back gave us a chance to read edifying books to each other and to have heart-to-heart talks. Ingrid was and still is a special treasure to me.

At Christmas each year we worked with the staff from the hospital for people with disabilities to do a Christmas party with them. The residents of the place really enjoyed the annual event and the hospital staff appreciated it too. At that time, people with disabilities were often not highly valued in Japan, but hidden away in remote places. As I think back to all the preparation that went into each year's celebration, I realize again how much the Japanese people love details.

God again gave me so many treasures here in this place.

Teine

In Teine, then a part of Sapporo City, I worked with Teine Christian Church as they laboured to start a daughter church, Izumi Christian Church. The first year I lived and worked with Magda from Switzerland. She made delicious Swiss chocolate cake using bread crumbs instead of flour and baking powder. Very delicious! After Magda went back to Switzerland I lived and worked with Nitta san, a believer from the Teine Christian Church. This was my first time to live and work full time with a Japanese person who spoke no English.

I learned about many Japanese ways and customs that I was unfamiliar with.

The pastor from the mother church, Pastor Masuda, volunteered many hands-on hours to the work of this new church plant. We met weekly for fellowship, sharing and a time of prayer. Another believer, Mr Yoshii, was a fireman who was able to give many hours to our work. His practicality and skills were much appreciated when we had to do renovations in the meeting hall downstairs. The pastor's wife, Shizuko, also helped me with how to teach and lead seekers in the study of God's Word. The mother church also sent two of their key people to join our work and serve with us. Seeing these folks give their all to the Lord and His work taught me so many things.

This church plant gave us the opportunity to make Christ known in many different ways, like cooking classes, English conversation classes, kids' club, concerts, etc. The church was always looking for ways to be involved. The believers in the mother church prayed fervently for us. If we had any needs, they were ready to think them through with us. At one point they decided they should buy their pastor a new car, but it did not stop there. Someone spoke up and said, "Then we should buy a new car for the daughter church as well." That was the first time in my life I had a brand new car to drive!

To this day, Teine church does not fear new beginnings and new things. If an opportunity opens to share the gospel, they want to go through it. Their motto remains, "Let's pursue God's work with prayer moving forward together." What a precious treasure!

Eniwa

Eniwa was next to Chitose, Sapporo's main airport. As Eniwa had very few churches, Chitose church decided that they would like to start a church plant in Eniwa because 15 of their members lived there. These people would become the nucleus of the new church. They started looking for a facility they could use as a church building that would also provide accommodations for the church plant worker. They found just the place a seven-minute walk from the railway station, near downtown Eniwa and close to schools.

The building they found had been a construction company owner's home and office building. I went with Pastor Komido from Chitose church and Mr. Honjo to look at the building. It was just what we needed. There was a small kitchen and living area, a bedroom, a study, and a half-bath upstairs, with the shower and bath downstairs. We could use the first floor for all our church activities. There was a large kitchen and dining area that we could use for cooking classes. The construction company's office would become our church sanctuary.

At the beginning we rented the place for 6 months. Eventually we decided that it could serve us better if we did some renovations, so we decided to buy the building. Pastor Komido and I went to the bank to make the loan, but the bank did not have $100,500 in cash on hand, so I had to go back later to pick it up. With the cash in hand I walked along the street, got in my car, drove to the construction owner's house, and handed over the money in cash. Never before had I carried around such a large amount of cash!

Right from the beginning, youth would often drop by the church after school. I recall twin sisters who were very keen to know the Lord. They had previously associated with the Mormons, but were dissatisfied with their experience there. They soon came to faith and brought along their friends.

We also had English classes, cooking classes, kids' club, and individual Bible studies for people who were interested. When we entered the third year in the building, we decided to build an addition to increase the size of the sanctuary. At that time, I called my friend Mrs. Ishigaki who lived in Kita Hiroshima. Her husband was a carpenter.

I asked her, "Do you think your husband would consider coming here and giving me some advice for adding onto our present building?" In the past he would run to the other side of the road to avoid the missionaries, but his heart had gradually softened. He had even built a bed for me to sleep on when I would come for a visit. When his wife asked him, he said, "Yes, I'll go." He carefully explained to me all the pros and cons and gave me his advice. It was hard to imagine that this could be the same man who had torn up his wife's Bible!

Komido sensei from the mother church was also very helpful in many ways. If we had things that we needed to discuss he would always make time for us.

One Friday night I did not know what was wrong with me. I had vomited at least 30 times in one night and I was in pain. As I had the kids' club at 1:30 and was responsible for the message, I thought I would rest as much as possible in the morning. Around 11:00 am Mr. & Mrs. Honjo came to help with setting up the room. I had not started anything. They were concerned and came upstairs to see if I was okay. They took one look at me and said they would go home to get something and then take me to the hospital.

When they came back, they had the money I would need for medical treatment. I went in for an x-ray and was told that I had appendicitis. It was dangerously close to bursting, so they had to do surgery immediately. Mr. & Mrs. Honjo called Komido sensei and told him about my situation. He left everything and came to the hospital immediately. We always talked in Japanese so I didn't even know that he could speak English, but that day he brought a small English New Testament with the Psalms. Before I was taken into surgery, he read some verses to me from Psalms and prayed with me in English! I felt so blessed and comforted that he would care for me in this way. Through seeing and receiving his pastoral care in different circumstances I gained the treasure of servant leadership.

In Eniwa I was also taught to wait patiently on the Lord as I taught people His Word. One day Yayoi, a young Christian lady, came to me and said she was dating a non-Christian. I encouraged her to bring him along to church and suggested that we do a Bible study together so he could find out for himself about the faith that was so important to Yayoi. He agreed to come and the first time we met was on his birthday. I baked a birthday cake for him, decorated it, and we celebrated together. After studying together for two full years he finally came to faith. Was it worth this kind of long-term investment? Absolutely yes! Today they have a Christian home and their oldest son is in Bible college preparing for full-time ministry. Japanese Christian author Miura Ayako said, "Where much care and attention has been lavished, there affection and commitment is born." How true. Learning this was another precious treasure I gained.

Asahikawa

In Asahikawa, Midori ga Oka Christian Church was the sixth church where I served. I was there 22 years in all. That was my longest placement with OMF. The church was near the Asahikawa National Medical

University. Siegfried Schnabel and his wife, the couple who pastored the church before handing it over to me, hoped that I would lead the church to call their first Japanese pastor. Since most of my experience in church planting was with Japanese co-workers, and I had a lot of experience with handing a church over to a Japanese pastor, they thought I would be perfect for the job. One year before I came to this church, they built a new church building. Siegfried and his wife, the couple who pastored the church before me both taught many hours of English classes to help pay off the loan. I was only one person. I told the church at the outset that I would not be able to do all the church work and additional work to pay off the loan. This church had never had any collection baskets passed around, so a number of people in the church did not have much concern for giving. A number of Japanese pastors who had spoken at the church over the years encouraged me to have a weekly giving time in the worship. When I arrived, there was a basket in the back, but often it was removed so quickly after the worship service that if you had stopped to talk to someone after the service, you missed the opportunity to give.

Therefore, early on in my ministry in this church, I did a two-session seminar on giving. During the course of the seminar I made sure there was considerable time for people to express what they were thinking. In the end it was agreed that we should have a time of giving in our worship services. The giving in our little church increased considerably. Instead of paying for our church building in seven years we paid it off in three! The church was thrilled to see what they had been able to do and continued to give generously for the many projects we had. Another big project funded through giving was paving our parking lot.

Since our church was near the university, many students came to our worship services as well. I helped with a Bible study on campus at the request of one of the students, which gave me a chance to build relationships with them. If students showed interest, I would encourage them to take an eight-week seekers course. As most of them had never held a Bible in their hands or heard a Christian message, they were usually quite keen to do so. After this eight-week introductory course, I asked them if they would like to continue studying the Bible. Most said yes. It was so encouraging to see them come to faith and go on to baptism, and then to become active in serving in the church.

At the beginning I went on campus to help with the Bible study, but after some time we changed the format and invited the students to come to my home. I would make a meal for them and afterward we would have a Bible study together. Usually, 15 to 20 students would come to these meals.

Somehow I had never considered that one-by-one after graduation the students would move away. For me it felt like children leaving home. I realized that I needed to make a switch in my thinking: It's not that the students are leaving us, but we are sending them out! This changed my attitude considerably. No longer would I look to them to join and help us, but rather we would prepare them to be their best for God wherever they were going.

Another outreach we had was for young moms and their children aged 1–3. This class was called mama/chibi meaning "mommy and toddler." This class was a highlight for the mothers and their little ones. Most of the children had no brothers or sisters, so this was their first place to experience community life. We arranged the church like a day care with a big jungle gym in the middle and theme carpets around the room. One carpet had puzzles, another had plush toys, another had picture books, another had toys like tractors, trucks, etc. In the kitchen we had a low table for playing house, with a child's kitchen: cutting boards, fruits & vegetables, and so forth. Each month we had a theme that we requested the mothers work on with their children. For example, one month was greetings. They should be able to say hello when they come in. They should also learn to say thank you and good-bye. Another month the theme would be sharing or learning to say thank you and so forth. We also had a very simple English time with the children. The last 15 minutes we would have a snack for the children and a Bible time for the mothers. Sadly, as more and more mothers started working outside the home, we stopped this class after six years.

Midori ga Oka Church was very different from other churches where I had worked. Usually, a missionary worked for four years and then had a Home Assignment for one year. Since we were planning to call a Japanese pastor after four years, I introduced the topic toward the end of my third year there. There was a strong request by key members in the church that I should become the pastor. At first I laughed it off and ignored it. I would bring up the plan to call a Japanese pastor again the next month, but again they would counter my suggestion with the same response: "No, we want you as our pastor." I was surprised but also honoured that they would even consider such a thing.

After the fifth time, my co-worker Conny from Germany said, "Don't you think about it at all when they bring it up so often?"

"No, I don't," I said.

The next day was my day off. I was at a hot spring relaxing and thinking about the talk the day before. Suddenly it came to me, Why don't I pray about it and get a 'no' from God and then I can tell them it is not God's will? So, I started to pray about it. Gradually my heart started to change. Maybe my serving as pastor would be a good way to do it. I could continue serving in the same church.

I had a chance to talk to Patrick, a missionary from another mission, who was doing just that. He had come up from Osaka to help us with an outreach meeting. He heard my Japanese and saw my interaction with the people who came. Later he said, "I think you could do it. You would be able to cope language-wise and culturally as well." Some of our OMF leadership were initially against it, but as leadership changed it was suggested we go ahead with it on a trial basis.

After that there was a period of intense testing. Criticism and gossip about me as pastor came out into the open. Just at that time I was reading a book on spiritual warfare and how Satan will try to destroy the church and often attack the spiritual leaders in the church. Through that book I was reminded of how insistent Satan is to get leaders down. I committed myself to firmly stand on God's side and not give a foothold to the evil one. After my Bible reading each morning, I would spend an hour walking along the river praying and worshipping and seeking the Lord for His intervention. I thank God for the wonderful treasure of deep fellowship with Himself that He allowed me to taste during this time.

I am so thankful for the blessing and joy of walking with the brothers and sisters in the Lord in that place. I was able to fully participate in their lives through Bible studies, weddings, child dedications, funerals, etc. I am confident that the Lord will continue to bless this church. And He will continue to add new people to their congregation. I am thankful for each one who so faithfully and wholeheartedly serves the Lord there. I believe God will continue to use this church for His glory.

The people of this church are a treasure so big they won't even fit into the treasure chest.

Children's Overnight Camp

Church building paid off in three years rather than seven.

After two years of study, this young man came to faith.
This photo was taken at the couple's engagement.

Handing off to a Japanese pastor.

Makino + Izu my older brother and older sister as we started our missionary careers together.
Izu edited my Japanese book.

Treasures Gained Through Difficulties

When Things Didn't Go as Planned

"Though the fig tree does not bud and there are no grapes on the vines, though the olive crop fails and fields produce no food, though there are no sheep in the pen and no cattle in the stalls, yet I will rejoice in the LORD, I will be joyful in God my Saviour." (Habakkuk 3:17-19)

"It's hopeless! Nothing is going as hoped."

As a missionary team we met for our weekly meeting. We were on the verge of giving up. We had worked hard to have good relationships with the people that we met. At the Tuesday night English class one of the junior high boys had his new bicycle stolen. Markus, a fellow worker, drove around town to try and find it, but it was futile. After two hours of searching with the young fellow they decided to go to the police and file a theft report. The bicycle was never found. Would the parents now decide that it was not safe to go the church?

Around the same time one of the Christian mothers called to say, "I won't be coming to the church anymore." She had tried to teach her children well but her son, who had come to faith, was giving in to temptation and she was embarrassed by his behavior. I had spent hours with both of them but she was tired. We as a team were so discouraged. We hurled our discontent and grumbling to the Lord Jesus Himself.

"Look. We have done everything we can. There is no use going on."

Maybe we hadn't heard the Lord clearly about how we were to move forward. Starting a new church plant meant that each person stood out. Family and friends were watching to see their next moves. Since Japan is basically Buddhist and Shinto, the Japanese people held Christianity at arm's length. How would it interfere with their customs and culture? Even our core group of church people were discouraged and tired.

It was in this kind of atmosphere that our weekly team meeting started. As good missionaries we started with prayer. Usually, we would read our Bible passage for the day and share what we felt God was saying to us. We would then check our activity plan for the year and then we would close with an extended time of prayer for each person. But that day our hearts were heavy and we could not concentrate to go beyond the opening prayer. One of the team members, Conny, said, "I think we should forget about our regular schedule and just spend our time worshipping the Lord in song." She got out her guitar and suggested the first song. Markus and Conny and I sang with heavy hearts, but gradually an amazing thing happened. After spending about 30 minutes praising the Lord and pouring out our hearts in song, the atmosphere began to change. The darkness that had hung over us was lifting. The circumstances had not changed but our outlook had! We knew that God was on the throne and that the work was His and not ours. In the end His joy was overflowing from our hearts.

That day we touched only briefly on the immediate activities before us. The rest of the time we spent worshipping and sharing how we had experienced God's grace and mercy to us. Our situation was just what Habakkuk talked about. Even though things on the surface didn't seem to be going well and there was nothing to show for our hard work, we chose to rejoice in the Lord and be joyful in Him. Hope and joy returned to our hearts. The precious treasures gained that day were a fresh appreciation for my fellow workers and a renewed love for the God who had called me to this ministry. Difficult things will happen, but God is still on the throne!

When Betrayed

"And we know that in all things God works for the good of those who love him, who have been called according to His purpose." (Romans 8:28)

It happened one Easter afternoon. Three key ladies in the church had asked to meet with our mission leader and me to discuss an issue they had with me. The mission leader asked if they had talked to me about it. They had not, but at their insistence he decided to come to the meeting. He gave me about half an hour notice that he was coming to pick me up to meet with the ladies. I wondered what it was all about. I depended on these ladies as they knew the history of the church. I was really puzzled.

Recently a seeker who had mental problems had been speaking negative things about these ladies when she came for her weekly Bible study. Each time, I tried to defend them, saying how they cared for people in the church. This seeker had quit coming because she was struggling with her mental health. When my mission leader and I got to the church, these women surrounded me and accused me of saying all the things about them that this mentally unstable individual had said. They went on to add what they perceived my motive to be. The things they accused me of had never even crossed my mind. I was shocked and speechless. I had promised the mentally unstable lady that I would not tell anyone what she had said. She specifically did not want these women to hear what she had said. When they confronted me, I was at a loss as to what to say. Should I defend myself? I decided that would be a breach of promise, so I replied only that I had not said the things they were accusing me of. I became angry with myself. Why had I even bothered defending these women, always speaking well of them when people complained to me? I was deeply hurt.

We had served the Lord together and one of the ladies had even said she wanted to quit her job early so that she could work as my secretary. And now this. In my experience in church work I felt that the Lord had blessed me with good relationships and that my work was a gift from Him. So, what was this all about? For about three months after that experience, I would go for an hour long walk every morning and pour my heart out to the Lord. I asked the Lord to somehow bring a conclusion to this misunderstanding and to bring about restoration. I even dreamt of how this would happen.

This whole thing was such a burden to me. I thought that if even an ounce of what these ladies were saying was true then I was not suitable to be God's servant. I was ready to throw in the towel. However, a part of me still felt that the Lord had a work for me do. I began to ask the Lord for confirmation that He really still had a work for me to do in Japan. Otherwise, I would return to Canada and stop my missionary career. Everything was laid bare before Him.

"Please show me clearly what You want me to do. What is Your will for me? If You want me to continue then I ask that You would allow me to see fruit in my labors for You."

At the end of that year as I looked back, I could only marvel at God's goodness and care for me. Certainly, He had answered my prayer. That year the Lord gave me the joy and the privilege of leading seven people to faith and discipling them as His children. The Lord did still have a work for me to do!

Even so, I still had deep pain over the incident. At that time, I was reading in 2 Timothy 1:15, "You know that everyone in the province of Asia has deserted me." Even in the life of Jesus Christ himself, all His disciples deserted Him. I was also reading a book that spoke of spiritual warfare as we serve our Lord. I tried to reason with myself and accept that this kind of experience was something any of us could face. However, it was not easy!

For a while I found it hard to trust people. My antenna was always up. Was what was being said really true? After a considerable time, I also knew that the Lord could use this whole experience as a special tool to instruct me further and mould me to be more like Christ. I realized that I had a sin in my life—pride. This sin held me back from becoming more Christlike. He led me to repentance and restored to me the joy and freedom of serving Him. After that, my healing continued little by little. Since then, I have forgiven those women and I can leave it all in God's hands.

This whole experience was a treasure that taught me more of the wonder of God's grace. I also received the treasure of knowing God's ways on a much deeper level. He will often use the painful things in life to take us deeper in His ways. No experience is useless and pointless. God works through them all. He is good.

When I Hit the Wall of My Own Limits

"For by the grace given to me I say to every one of you; Do not think of yourself more highly than you ought, but rather think of yourself with sober judgement, in accordance with measure of faith God has given you." (Romans 12:3)

When I was in Eniwa, I had appendicitis and a complicated fracture on my left ankle. On my ankle alone I had three surgeries. In the church, too, there were numerous challenges and I began to feel that I had no breathing space. Physically I felt tired, mentally I felt tired, and spiritually I felt drained. I had no energy left. When I came back to Canada on Home Assignment, I felt I needed to learn to take better care of myself. If I continued at the rate I was going, I would face burnout and would not be able to continue in missionary work. I decided that first of all I would start a walking program. I walked 6.5 km every day. It was refreshing and invigorating to spend time walking in the fresh air each day. I noticed a significant change in my energy levels. This was a very good therapy for me.

It is not my nature to do the bare minimum when I set to a task. I challenge myself to do the best job I possibly can and always strive to improve myself. To do this in our own strength can become very wearing and tiring. On the other hand, if we can do things in our own strength, we won't need faith. Zechariah 4:6 has always been an encouragement to me: "'Not by might, nor by power, but by my Spirit,' says the Lord Almighty." As I walk in step with the Holy Spirit and He has His way to work freely in my life, the burden is lightened considerably.

That year I came home so worn out even my parents became concerned. I had a period when I did not want to see anyone and just hid away in my room. However, as my rhythm changed and I allowed myself to rest, my outlook also changed. After taking some time to rest and restore my spirit, things started to look more encouraging and my perspective began to change. I even took up tole painting that year. Another key factor in my recovery process was being quiet before the Lord. I set aside longer periods of time to read God's Word, meditate, journal, read faith-related books, and pray. If life is just push, push or go, go, then eventually problems emerge. During that year I learned some important lessons on balancing my life of service with living for Christ and walking daily with Him.

Through that year of struggles and confusion God showed Himself to me in special ways. The greatest treasure I gained was the joy of walking with Him, loving Him and sharing all of my life with Him. He became my joy and anchor in a new and fresh way.

Building relationship with neighbourhood men through park golf

Treasures Gained Through Seeing God at Work

Turning to God in Their Final Hours

"For God so loved the world that He gave His one and only Son, that whoever believes in Him shall not perish but have eternal life." (John 3:16)

How could a man like this ever come to meet Jesus Christ as his personal Saviour? Mr. Yuhara was a high school teacher. He loved his job and he loved to be in charge. His wife had come to faith in Jesus Christ through their daughter. When Mrs. Yuhara came to faith, her daughter told her, "You need to go to church on Sundays" and suggested that she come to our church because it was nearest to her mother-in-law, whom she cared for on a regular basis.

Mr. Yuhara was not interested in church, but since his daughter and his wife both insisted that the wife go to church, he decided to go along with it. At the beginning he would not bring her all the way to church, but rather dropped her off at the nearest intersection. After a couple of months, he decided to drop her off at the driveway entrance to the church parking lot, as she always seemed to have a lot to carry. In Japan we always had lunch together after our Sunday worship service. She would always bring different dishes she had prepared, so she really did have a lot to carry. After bringing his wife that far for a few weeks, he decided to drive into the church parking lot and drop her off at the door. As time passed his wife began asking for rides to the church during the week. She would often help with different outreaches like Alpha course, children's outreaches, and so forth, but he always stayed outside.

One day I asked Mrs. Yuhara, "Do you think your husband would be prepared to put up curtain rods and build a mailbox center for the church?"

"I don't know," she said.

"Okay how about we ask him if he would be willing to fix a terrace door rail at my house first?" I asked. The threshold for a church building is very steep for many Japanese people.

She said, "I'll ask him."

Amazingly, he agreed to come if he could bring his friend and fellow teacher with him. I was happy for that. They even stayed for tea after they had finished the task. A few weeks later his wife Toshiko asked him if he would be able to put up curtain rails and build a mail center for the church. He was not sure at first. She said she would ask me to be there to explain it to him. He agreed to come on one condition; that no church believers would be there. Only me, the sensei, and his wife. We agreed. Finally, he had come into the church building and even looked around a bit. After another six months or so, he would drop off his wife and then go to 7-Eleven to buy us each a lunch and we would eat together in the church. It took about two years before he was willing to meet any believers. He did not want anyone to talk to him about the Lord. He usually tried to steer the conversation to places that he felt safe in.

About eight years later he went for a regular cancer check, as he was a survivor. The results of that appointment shocked him and his wife.

That evening Mrs. Yuhara called me and said, "Sensei, would you please come to the hospital and see my husband? He has one to two weeks left to live. I would like you to share the gospel with him in a clear and simple way."

I agreed to go see him the following afternoon.

I went to his bedside and held his hand. He was quite drugged and limp. I told him that his wife had asked me to come and talk to him. I said, "You know she really wants you to know the Lord Jesus. But we cannot know Jesus unless we humble ourselves and realize that we have lived our lives according to our own desires rather than God's standards. This has caused a big rift between us and God our creator. Someone who had obeyed God fully was needed to take our place and die for our sin. Jesus did that on the cross. He had no sin but He died for us. He died for you. Do you know that you are a sinner and that Jesus died for you?"

"Yes, I do," he said.

"Would you like to thank Him for dying for you and trust Him as your own Saviour?"

His voice was weak, but he responded, "Yes," and squeezed my hand. I prayed and asked him to make it his own prayer if he meant it.

"Thank you, Father, that you created me and have a wonderful plan for my life. I have lived life my own way. Please forgive my sin. Thank you that Jesus died on the cross for me. I give my life to you. Thank you for welcoming me as your child."

"Amen."

His wife and daughter were standing nearby. When they heard his firm "Amen" they hugged each other and jumped together for joy. I told them that I would come again the next day. That evening Toshiko called me and thanked me for talking straightforwardly with her husband.

"Would you be willing to baptize him when you come tomorrow?" she asked.

I said, "I would like to make sure he understands, but if that is what he wants, I am willing to baptize him."

The next day when I walked into the room, he held out his hand and smiled.

Then he said to me, "I was at the church yesterday."

"What did you see at church?" I asked.

"The children were happy and were hugging and dancing."

"Really?" I asked. "Did you see Aika? (his favorite child at church) or was it maybe your daughter and your wife?"

"Oh," he sighed and then dozed off for a while.

When he opened his eyes again, I asked him "Mr. Yuhara, do you know that you are a sinner and need Jesus?"

"Yes" he said.

Then I asked him, "Do you trust Him as YOUR Saviour?"

"Yes," he said.

"And do you want to be baptized and confess Him as your Saviour and Lord?"

"Yes," he said without wavering.

I baptized him and three weeks later he went to be with Jesus. I visited him every day and gave him a verse and a few words of encouragement.

I wondered what the family would do for a funeral. His siblings were all very opposed to Jesus Christ. When I met with the family to plan the funeral service, his daughter firmly told the family. "My mother and I saw how my father came to trust Jesus as his Saviour and we want to honor his desire to follow Christ and give him a Christian burial."

One brother still tried to take over, but then Mr Yuhara's friend, who was also a school teacher, said to the siblings, "In a situation like this it is better to follow the wishes of the wife and daughter who are the immediate family." The siblings gave in and we had a Christian funeral. During the wake, the younger brother of Mr. Yuhara made a scene holding up his Buddhist scroll.

I found it hard to preach in that environment. When I got home, I prayed to God saying, "Father, I cannot go on and do the funeral and other services tomorrow if the family opposes so blatantly." The next day, to my surprise the family all walked in late for the funeral service and so they had to take the seats in the back. I was able to rest in the Lord for the services at the crematorium and the thanksgiving afterward. I praised God for showing His victory in a very difficult situation and for giving me freedom to speak God's Word freely in the circumstances.

What a treasure to see God work in such a powerful way in and through the life of Mr. Yuhara.

Now let me introduce you to Granny Suzuki. She was in the hospital, unconscious, and had not responded to anyone for two full days.

Her granddaughter called me and said, "Sensei, please go and see my granny. I am on my way, but it will take at least three hours as the roads are icy."

I went to the hospital and found that things were just as I had been told. Granny was unresponsive. I held her hand, gently massaging it, and read John 3:16 aloud and prayed with her. Her eyelid twitched. Then I sang quietly, "What a friend we have in Jesus" in Japanese. An amazing thing happened. She opened her eyes wide and looked at me. The nurse came in and was so surprised and immediately took her blood pressure. It was fine. After that I went every day for five days. I had Christmas and year-end activities that I needed to prepare for. Right after the New Year I would be going back to Canada for three weeks, so after the New Year's service I asked Mrs. Suzuki's son-in-law, who was a seeker in our church at the time, what they would do for a funeral if his mother-in-law passed away.

"Oh we would have a Sokka Gakkai funeral the same as her husband had."

Sokka Gakkai is very strong Buddhist sect.

I said to him, "It might be good to ask your mother-in-law what she would like, as she is clearly believing in Jesus."

So right after the service he went to the hospital to see her. "When you die, it is best to have your funeral at the Sokka Gakkai the same as your husband, right?" he asked.

"Oh no," she said. "I want the Christian pastor to do it. She loves me and cares for me and comes to visit me."

An hour or so later he called me and said, "I can't believe it, but she wants you to do the funeral. She asked to be baptized. Would you be able to do that today? Our daughter and her family will leave again today, so, it would be good if we could do it when we are all together."

I said, "Yes. I will be there in about half an hour."

Granny Suzuki was filled with joy and praise and confessed Jesus Christ as her Lord and Saviour. Even her 22-year-old grandson who was not a Christian, said, "That was beautiful. She was so happy. Thank you for coming."

The next day I explained to Granny that I was going back to Canada for three weeks. "If all of a sudden things take a turn for the worse and you go to be with Jesus, then I will ask my friend Pastor Komido to do your funeral."

Well, that was not necessary. She waited till I got back. Five days after my return she went to be with the Lord.

I've known numerous others like these two who came to know Jesus in their final hour. They are special treasures that God gave to me.

When Prayer Was Answered

"They were helped in fighting them ... because they cried out to Him during the battle. He answered their prayers, because they trusted in Him." (1 Chronicles 5:20)

Hiroko had hepatitis B. While she was pregnant, she lost a lot of blood and had to have a blood transfusion. She contracted hepatitis B through an infected needle. Since then, she had been to many hospitals to get the best medical treatment possible. Her husband was a doctor and so he felt a special responsibility to give her the best.

One day I had a call from her husband, asking me if I would please go and see his wife as she was asking for me. I was in hospital myself with a complicated ankle surgery. It was one hour by taxi to get to her hospital. My ankle nerves were very sensitive and so my doctor decided to shield them with Styrofoam wraps. The only stipulation from my doctor was that I would go by taxi and be back in four hours.

When I got to Hiroko's room, she started to cry. I could tell immediately that the tears were not sad tears, but tears of joy. She told me the reason for her joy. For her next medical procedure she needed to swallow a scope. They had tried to do it three times in two days but each time she would gag and they could go no further. The doctor had told her the night before, "We will try the test one more time tomorrow morning. If it does not work, we can't do anything further and we will send you home."

Frustrated and completely at her wits end, Hiroko prayed. Jesus himself came to visit her and appeared to her in person. He showed her His nail-pierced hands, so she knew it was really Him. He spoke to her and said, "Hiroko, I died for you by being nailed to the tree. This was so that you could be healed. You too need to give yourself for your family even if it is very difficult." After that she saw her husband and their three children in the distance. Through Jesus' words she received courage and decided that when they came again for the test, she would give it her best, so she prayed, "Lord Jesus, please help me in my weakness. I will give it my all and do the best I can." That evening she slept like a babe. In the morning she felt well-rested and ready for her day. The medical procedure was a success!

This experience gave her new confidence in Christ and His care for her. She said to me, "I want to follow Christ and be baptized as soon as possible." She asked me, "Would you please explain my faith to my husband and my desire to follow Jesus?"

I prayed for the right timing to meet her husband. After I was released from hospital, I went to his hospital pretending I needed some medication. When I told him that his wife had asked me to talk to him, he asked his nurse assistant to leave. I told him how Hiroko had come to faith and the experience of seeing Jesus that she had had in hospital. I also explained that she wanted to be baptized. He looked at me and said, "If that is what Hiroko wants then I want to make sure that becomes a reality." He arranged for her to be moved to his hospital. She told him herself what was on her heart and that she really wanted to be baptized. He said he would arrange it. She has since gone to heaven to be with her Saviour, Jesus Christ. In Japan it is often the case that people are so busy that they have no room for Christ until their time is limited and they face the unknown future. Hiroko's faith and love for Jesus made her a beautiful treasure to behold.

Note: In Japan, ceremonies are very important. Baptism is not necessary for salvation, but in Japanese culture, a ceremony confirms the decision made. As long as people have not been baptized, family and friends will assume that they can still back out of their commitment. So, for a person to gain credibility before family and friends, following through with the baptism ceremony is very important.

When the Impossible Became Possible

"Call to me and I will answer you and tell you great and unsearchable things you do not know." (Jeremiah 33:3)

For God's thoughts and plans to become a reality, He sometimes does amazing things that are beyond our understanding. This is a story of one of those times when He answered our prayers in the most amazing way.

In 1977, we were in a housing development that did not allow for any religious buildings like churches and temples. We were two single missionaries and six local believers. Four of the believers were less than two years old in their faith. We had tried in so many ways to make Christ known. We would get outside help to deliver gospel tracts to every home in town in a single day. We had a weekly Bible study for women and a club for elementary school age children. We also had special events like one-day workshops with guest speakers, a movie night, and monthly come-and-go days of prayer.

Around that time, a man from the local town office came to us for help in translating for a girl from Alberta who was working on his farm. In exchange, he offered to help us. He could see that we really needed a place from which to work, so he came by with this proposal:

"We are starting the fourth and final kindergarten allowed for this housing development. It is impossible for you to get a church building for at least ten years, but if you started a kindergarten, then you could have a room for the church inside the kindergarten building. The town requires that the kindergarten must be big enough to accommodate 120 children."

He gave us that concrete and detailed information wanting to spur us on to move ahead with the project. But what could we do? We were six women and two men. Three of the women had non-Christian husbands who were very opposed to their faith. We called a meeting and presented what we had been told to the six believers.

We said, "At this time we are not asking you to make a decision, but we are asking you to pray. Pray that the Lord would show us any big gaps this could bring that would make us less effective for the gospel. Also pray that if God wants us to move forward with the project, He would open the doors for us and if this isn't in His will that He would close the doors." If God would not work miracles, it would bring disgrace and shame to His name.

After three weeks of praying, we came together to share the impressions that God had put on our hearts. When we met again nobody said, "Oh that is too big a task for us," but rather, "If God continues to open the doors, then we should move forward." Our application had to include the following documents: a blueprint of the floor plan, the name and personal history of a potential kindergarten principal, and proof that we had the 20,000,000 yen for the project (about $200,000 USD). Additionally, we had to have the names and brief backgrounds of the people who would compose our board of directors.

Humanly speaking, this was impossible for our little group, but as we looked around and prayed, we realized first of all that one of our missionaries from England was an architect. We also realized that one of the pastors in our church organization, Pastor Hosokawa, had experience working in Tokyo in a church that ran a church kindergarten. Pastor Hosokawa suggested that we not decide on a long-term kindergarten principal at this stage but rather find one who would temporarily fill that position. Pastor Hosokawa and our OMF director in Japan, along with two church members and one Christian in the community, were willing to work as board members. This left only the money, but where on earth would we get that? It seemed the lack of money would be what would halt the project.

The local town council man who originally came to us with this proposal came from time to time to see how we were progressing. When he'd ask if we had sent the application in yet we always had to say no. We did not want him to know that the lack of money was what kept us from moving forward. Just days before the application was due, he came again. This time he said, "Look, if it's a lack of money that is stalling you then please, no more holding back. I will underwrite you financially." We could hardly believe our ears. Had we heard right? We had. He took care of all the paperwork from his end. We had all our papers ready to submit the application. Out of 14 applicants, ours was the one accepted. You can imagine the joy and excitement we felt as we looked forward to what the Lord had ahead for us.

Shortly after we were accepted, we found out that the man was not standing by us with his own money but with his wife's inheritance money. And to make it even worse he had done it in secret. We told him that we did not need his money. Soon after that we learned that since we would be receiving some grant money from the Hokkaido government, it had to be a government architect who drew up the blueprints. Of course, we had known from the start that the principal was just a temporary find. We were again completely dependent on the Lord and He miraculously provided exactly what we needed. People around the world had heard about this kindergarten project and started to give. Churches in Switzerland, England, Canada, and throughout Japan, began to give. Our own church people who were able gave their houses as collateral for a loan. In the end all the money came in. Advertising among our churches helped us find a principal, four teachers, and one office staff person (all believers) to start our first year on April 1, 1978. God had worked a miracle! We knew that He had a task for us to do in the days ahead and He would bless it.

Nothing is impossible for our God. He works beyond what we can think or imagine. For me it was truly exciting to take part in these adventures in my first term of ministry 47 years ago. God is good!

Teaching with my puppet

Granny Suzuki's graveside ceremony at the communal church grave

Closing

"The Lord your God has chosen you out of all the peoples on the face of the earth to be his people, his treasured possession." (Deuteronomy 7:6)

How wonderful to know God's heart for all peoples that they become His treasured possession and also treasures to each other. I thank God for each of these treasures that He has brought into my life.

I close with one very personal treasure. I was simultaneously working as director for Hokkaido OMF and pastoring a church in Asahikawa. My work as director involved living in Sapporo from Monday to Thursday to work in the office and travel around the island visiting missionaries in their times of need. My work as pastor involved doing church work in Ashahikawa from Thursday night to Monday: preparing my message for Sunday, having meetings and consultations that I needed to catch up on.

One Thursday in April, we had an unexpected snowfall. I decided to put off returning to Asahikawa till Friday morning, hoping all the snow would have melted. One stretch of road was very slushy and treacherous. The slush was pulling on my front tires. I was behind a very slow driver, so I decided to overtake him when the unthinkable happened! My front tires got sucked into the slush rut and I lost complete control. I was heading straight toward the meridian. I said to the Lord, "Father, I'm coming home!" I heard the metal crunch under my car as I hit the meridian, but something amazing happened. God sent His angel. He lifted up my car, turned it around 180 degrees and giving me a push from behind, saying, "Do not stop. Keep going." It was not an audible voice, but in my heart it was loud and clear. I kept going, straight back into the traffic. A big dump truck had stopped to let me in. As he passed me, he bent forward to catch a glimpse of me. I often wonder what he had seen. After driving for one and half hours, I saw a place for a washroom break and I needed to stop. My first thought was, Have I gone far enough without stopping? What if the metal is so crunched that I can't close the door if I open it? But I really did need the break.

I stopped and opened the door. To my surprise, it opened smoothly. I got out and looked around the car. I could not see a single scratch. God had protected me.

I am His treasure and He has sustained me, kept me, and given me all I needed to serve Him. Truly we are chosen to be His treasured possessions and He delights to bless us and use us for His glory. All praise and glory to His name.

Phlox Moss - Shiba Zakura bw

Acknowledgements

I want to thank the many people who have helped me in the writing of this book. They have been a real encouragement and make me look good.

First of all, Pastor Komido in Japan, who I worked with in two different churches, encouraged me to write the book in the first place. In a busy schedule I did not think I had time for it, but in the end the Lord made it clear that I should do it. Pastor Komido also helped me with getting the book to the printer.

My friend Izu Makino edited the book in Japanese and gave me many helpful leads along the way. Thank you, Makino Sensei, for volunteering your wife for the job.

Prayer supporters and financial supporters were telling me they would like to read the book, too. With COVID interruptions I had the extra time to give to the task of translating the book into English. Thank you for your encouragement.

After I compiled my manuscript, the following beta readers—Allan Dueck, Eleanor Braun, Susan Warne, and Ann Timonin—made indispensable contributions to this book. Thank you so much.

Finally, I want to thank Colleen, Charity, Susan, and Travis at Siretona Creative for the help you have been in the publishing process. Without Colleen's direction and help this would not have become a reality. Thank you so much to all of you.

Author Biography

Ruth Dueck worked in Japan for 42 years with OMF International. She was involved in six church plants, working under the leadership of Japanese pastors in three of them. She came back to Canada in 2016 and works with Diaspora Returnee Ministry to reach out to Japanese students who come to Winnipeg for study.

Learn more about Ruth at her webpage:
https://www.siretona.com/dueck-treasures/

www.ingramcontent.com/pod-product-compliance
Lightning Source LLC
Chambersburg PA
CBHW071423070526
44578CB00003B/668